Sunshine For The Pessimist

Cas Potterton

BookLeaf Publishing

India | USA | UK

Presentation by *BookLeaf Publishing*

Web: www.bookleafpub.com

E-mail: info@bookleafpub.com

ISBN: 978-93-5744-347-0

First edition 2022

DEDICATION

To those who always believed that I could,

And to spite those who ever said I couldn't.

ACKNOWLEDGEMENT

None of this would ever have been possible without:
My superhero of a mum, who has always been my biggest fan.
My girlfriend Chloe, who has served as an excellent muse more times than I can count.
Miss Roberts, who ignited my love of poetry in the first place.

I'm also obliged to acknowledge Miss Bakunowicz, who once told me she'd always wanted to be mentioned in a book.

Thank you all.

There Is No Shame In Love

I'm no stranger to dark thoughts
On cold nights,
When the windowsill is so enticing,
And the concrete looks so soft.

I know how hard it is
To stop and smell the flowers,
When you know
Your hopes and dreams are pushing daisies.

I've walked the cliff edge of despair:
A gust of wind away
From tumbling down the darkened rabbit hole,
Teetering gently,
As if the plummet is no big deal.

And I did plummet...
Down a spiral staircase with no end,
Down and down.
Each step stealing the warmth from my hands,
And the hope from my heart:
Overcome by numbness.

I thought I'd never stop tumbling.
For years I believed I'd never break the cycle,

Of silent tears and self-destruction,
Confusion and chaos.

But I was wrong.
Because eventually the seemingly endless fall
slowed and stopped.
Eventually I had the strength to stand.
A stair at a time I began to climb.
I scaled my own hopelessness.
I crawled out of the hell I'd been prematurely
damned to,
And I owe it all,
To love...

I know surviving yourself is not a walk in the
park,
And a walk in the park won't cure your
depression,
But fuck anyone who says there's no hope.
Because some things in life are still worth
getting excited about.

There is no shame in love.
Love for that book you've read 43 times.
Because you see yourself in that one character,
Who is just as flawed as the rest of us,
But saves the world nonetheless.

Love for that song you've had on repeat for 3
weeks.
Because you can lose yourself in the syncopated
rhythms
That match the irregular beating of your heart,
And find peace in the voice of someone
Who finally found a way to put your feelings
into words.

Love for that show that was on stage for 2
weeks.
The one you saw twice and will never see again,
But will never let go of,
Because your childhood love of Robin Hood
never really died...
Because the story set a fire down in your soul,
And you haven't stopped smiling since.

Love,
Is a very powerful thing...
You'd do wisely not to underestimate it,
Because love can save a life.
Be it the warmth of a mother's hug,
Or a partner's kiss,
Or words that you hold to your heart so
delicately:
From that book,
That song,
That show...

There is no shame in love.
Because we have one life,
One soul,
One heart.
And as long as mine is bursting with
Adulation,
Admiration,
Adoration!
As long as I know love,
I am alive and kicking.

Harmless Fireworks

Fireworks.
Harmless fireworks.
Each bang, pop, and squeal:
Merely the violent by-product of seemingly
celestial artwork.
God's great paintbrush streaking coloured sparks
across the night sky:
Lingering just for a moment before the canvas
dramatically fades to black once more.
Harmless fireworks.
Each bang, pop, and squeal:
Ringing in your ears as wide eyes flicker with
childlike wonder.
Each intricate pattern expertly woven:
A heavenly tapestry in view for mortal beings to
enjoy.

Harmless fireworks.
Each bang, pop, and squeal:
Another bullet barely dodged as blood is spilled
on the barricade,
A crimson river through the cobbled street.
Red flags raised high in defiance but the
situation is dire.
Harmless fireworks.

Each bang, pop, and squeal:
Either a victory or defeat as neither side seems
to have an advantage.
Until a flickering torch is held threateningly
against a barrel of gunpowder.
Enemy forces flee but the fight is far from
finished,
As each school boy tends to their wounds and
mourns the friends who didn't make it.

Harmless fireworks.
Each bang, pop, and squeal:
A warning to run, sweet Jesus run for your life,
As great cylinders of destruction rain from the
sky,
Guaranteeing devastation wherever they land.
Mothers struggle to console screaming children
as they are enclosed in darkness,
Smoke filling their fragile lungs.
Harmless fireworks.
Each bang, pop, and squeal:
Followed by orders barked by tall men with
large guns, tired eyes,
And not an ounce of fear.
Frozen in place as you watch companions fly or
fall,
Ultimately doomed to die in a valley watered
with blood.

Harmless fireworks.
Each bang, pop, and squeal:
A score for the first black battalion as the
Americans fight for their land back.
Adrenaline so high the Sons of Liberty seem
invincible as they mow down their oppressors.
Harmless fireworks.
Each bang, pop, and squeal:
Another red-coat hitting the floor,
As their entrails paint pictures of independence
for the freedom fighters.
Britain fights a losing battle,
As the colonies take back what was rightfully
theirs in the first place!

Harmless fireworks.
Each bang, pop, and squeal:
Drags him back to a battle he never fought,
Yet the fright seems all too real.
He can feel the cockade pinned to his coat,
A rifle heavy in his freezing hands but to
onlookers he is just a dazed child.
Harmless fireworks.
Each bang, pop, and squeal:
Throws colours across the sky, awesome in all
respects.
Sandwiched between family and strangers
singing Auld Lang Syne,

Yet his attention is focused upwards at heaven's great lightshow.

"Happy New Year..."

Walking On Sunshine

I was done with dancing on eggshells.
Never knowing when the next explosion would
come,
Simply because you didn't get what you
wanted...
Simply because I refused to be your toy...

I was worth so much more than thin ice.
Not just your accessory,
Or some sort of device:
A scapegoat,
For the evil that came with the problems,
That made you too interesting to warrant getting
help for...

I'd had it with tip toeing around you.
Your fragile ego and unpredictable emotions:
A danger I never signed up for,
And thought I'd never escape...

I deserved to be walking on sunshine!

And that's where I am now.
No more egg shells,
No more thin ice,

No more tip toeing.
Just me, and my sunshine,
And the happiness I was so deprived of with
you...

So get it through your thick, fucking skull...
That's why I left.

Loving You Is Effortless

I never have to think twice
About the butterflies jackhammering my guts,
Or the flurry of fireworks exploding in my brain,
Or the heart palpitations that are just on the
happy side of cardiac arrest,
Because you are perfect.

We shared our first kiss late at night,
After a concert,
Covered in face paint,
And I was crying my eyes out.
We had been together for a year at this point,
And physically seen each other
For maybe 4 of those 365 days…
You had never kissed anyone before,
And kept telling me
You had no idea what you were doing,
But you were perfect.
And every time since has been perfect,
And I will never get bored of kissing you,
Because you are perfect.

Sometimes my meds make furniture melt.
And walls melt,
And floors melt,

And the air wobble like there's fire everywhere,
And it's terrifying.
When I lie with you –
Limbs intertwined and going numb –
Everything melts.
I don't know where I end and you begin,
But it's the opposite of terrifying,
Because you are perfect.

Eternity is a long, long time,
And gods know I'm afraid of the future
And the endless possibilities that forever holds.
But holy shit I want to be with you forever.
Still laughing over Joe Wilkinson when we're
83,
And drinking 7 cups of tea a day,
Until there's more milk and sugar in us than
blood,
Because you are perfect.

You make me want to take care of myself.
You make me want to stay on this god forsaken
planet.
You make me want to live another day,
And see a million tomorrows.
Even though I can't see you every day,
I live for you every day,
I love you every day,
Because you are perfect.

Thank you for enhancing my life
Beyond my wildest dreams –
And we know my dreams are certainly wild.
You allow me to live, laugh, and love
Like I never thought I could.

Loving you is effortless,
Because you are perfect.
X

All Your Faves Are Ace

Imagine if TV shows Favoured good
representation,
 Over frequent fornication.
 Or 'love' scenes in movies
Moved over,
Making room for Cluedo, or Kerplunk, or
Boggle.
Or maybe once in a while,
A book character's life wouldn't be governed by
coital desire.
Wouldn't it be refreshing to see
A character more like me:
Asexual.

And no,
I'm not a plant,
But even Audrey 2 had some odd attachments.
And no,
I'm not a robot,
But even Bicentennial Man wanted some action.
And even if I could reproduce alone,
It wouldn't affect this dire representation
situation,
Because I'm not so sure Plankton and Karen

Always kept it strictly PG...

4 in 52 cards are ace.
But did you know that
So are 1 in 100 people?
That makes it roughly a 2:1 ratio:
Gingers to aces,
So starting with the Weasleys,
We've got some catching up to do.

So I'm putting my foot down today.
I'm starting a revolution,
Ordering the execution of all the Barney
Stinsons on TV,
Making way for people like me:
Asexual.

Who says Newt Scamander can't have
A healthy, fulfilling life,
With his kids and his wife,
And still prefer majestic winged beasts
Over shuffling sheets?
I'm sure Castiel cares more
About the Apocalypse,
Than crashing hips,
Groot is more organic,
Less orgasmic,
The Doctor's more concerned about
regeneration

Than copulation,
And Eggin would rather have cake
Than sex.
That one doesn't rhyme but you get the gist.

We revolt at dawn,
No more silver screen porn!
I want Bake-Off to take centre stage,
I want dragons and theatre,
And a million things,
That are a million times more important,
To the 70 million of us,
To populate modern media...
In lieu of the message:
There's no love without sex.

And while we're at it,
I can't say I'd be devastated,
If the word 'sexy' was banned entirely,
Unless in reference to
Bass guitars, the TARDIS, or flawless
calligraphy.
Because let's face it,
It's weird that there's a word that communicates
—
In just two syllables –
That you want to get down and dirty with
someone...

Something has to be done,
And it begins right now.
Aces of all shapes, sizes, ages, and races,
Normal people with massive hearts,
Only sexual indifference sets us apart.
Not robots or aliens,
Not psychopaths or prudes.
I'm not 'waiting for the right person',
Because that's just not how it works.
And my hormones are fine,
Good,
Great in fact!
I'm just me.
Always have been,
Always will be!

Change will come,
And it starts right here.
With the Luna Lovegoods,
The Blake Belladonnas,
The Robin Hoods,
And the Sherlocks.
We'll ride forth on wyverns,
Wielding cake-pop katanas,
Let's paint the skies purple and grey,
Today's the day we say:

All your faves are ace,
And there's nothing you can do about it.

Social Situation

4, 5, 7, 8, 10, 11,
Or a dozen.
A quaint gathering at a table
Can feel like a packed-out stadium.
And friendly conversation,
Rather than simple social convention,
Is like performing to an audience.
Like a gladiator in a colosseum,
My fate decided based on performance:
Life and death over the quality of small talk.

In reality…
I've built a fort of beer mats and peanuts,
Blocking out twelve discussions,
A world of my own with a pen and pad,
Parma Violets, tiny croissants, Love Hearts, and
Frazzles.
The people fade out,
The noise is gone,
And Caesar slowly raises his thumb.

I successfully survived,
The Social Situation.

Leave My Art Out Of This

Go ahead and hate me.
Resent me for the things you claim I did,
Regardless of their legitimacy.
Publish your convoluted falsehoods to the
world;
To the witless few who still believe.
Call me dishonest, disloyal, unfaithful,
Conjure up crimes I've committed,
Copy and paste yourself into parts of my life
That never concerned you,
To make it seem as though
I wronged you in countless ways.
Paint me as the devil if you will…
I can't stop you,
And I no longer have the energy,
Nor the desire to try.

But don't you dare insult my craft.

Poetry is my art,
My way of spilling my soul
To those willing to listen.
When my emotions are set into stanzas,
I can help them understand what it's like up
here.

I can be open about what I love and hate,
What hurts me and what helps me.
It is not merely an excuse for malice,
And for you to excuse me of such is
unforgivable.
You are vile.
And sorely mistaken
If you think I'll stand for this slander…

Already you've stripped me of so much,
Until I was barely a shadow of my former self –
My happy self.
But I will not let this be taken from me.
You cannot soil the last pure thing in my life.
There is little I indulge in anymore,
For what once brought me joy,
Is now shrouded in darkness.
A friend once held a BB gun to my head,
And the shiver down my spine,
Mimicked that which arises,
When I walk past the park,
That was a massive part of my childhood,
And the same park you left me stranded in
After saying you were going to kill yourself,
And it was all my fault…
And not for the first or last time.

Poetry:
One of the few things you've yet to ruin

In such a manner.
It's held me together since I was twelve:
A constant in my life,
While you began tearing me apart
At barely fifteen years old.
I was forced to accept your hatred
Of my family,
My friends,
My interests,
My faith,
My transition.
And while it hurt
That you were never proud of my achievements,
I never voiced that hurt,
In an effort to keep you happy.
It wasn't until I began writing this,
That I finally realised.
What you really hated,
Was my individuality…

You'd think that would hurt too,
But it doesn't.
I'm now fully aware that what you really
wanted,
Was a non-sentient possession to dispense
attention,
Rather than a boyfriend:
A complex human being,

With thoughts and feelings and issues of his
own.
So rather than wasting any more time
Wallowing in sadness,
I'm filled with joy.
Yes,
Joy.
Really, I should thank you.

I write only truth,
Though I don't expect a pathological liar,
Such as yourself,
To believe that.
But know that every time you publicise
A new paragraph of misinformation,
That contradicts the last,
I'm struck by a wave of inspiration
That I can't get anywhere else.
We wouldn't have this very poem
If you hadn't announced that I was
A thieving, lying, attention-seeking cheater.
And I know that my way with words riles you
up,
So, let me reword what I said before.

Go ahead and hate me.
Resent me for the things you claim I did.
Publish your convoluted falsehoods to the world.
Paint me as the devil if you will.

But if I were you,
I'd stop fuelling this creative fire,
And leave my art out of this.

A Play To Change A Life

[My love letter to Winter In Sherwood]
I'm not always a happy chappy.
I'm sure that comes as no surprise,
Given the dullness in my eyes,
Or how often one of my OCs dies…
It all went to shit when I was 11,
Freshly flung into year 7,
Highschool was a battlefield,
And I was on the losing side,
Trust me I tried,
But I was forced to yield…

And I realise 10 lines into this poem,
That there was no way I could keep up this
rhyming,
And that this is far too much exposition,
So let's skip to the point:

Robin Hood changed my life…
800 years after he was offed by evil nuns,
In the form of an attractive uni student
And fifteen of his friends,
Jumping about a dramatically lit stage,
In the heart of Lincoln city.

It was a process that took two lots
Of two hours including interval,
12 days apart.
And let me tell you:
It was magical.

Winter In Sherwood was a short Christmas
adventure.
For hundreds of people?
Nothing more,
Nothing less.
Two hours of immersion that ended when it
ended.
But not for me.
Of course not.
I got attached to that show
Quicker than crabs to that one person we all
knew in year 10…

It's as if a switch was flicked in my funny little
brain,
And suddenly all I could think about
Was Merry Men, minstrels, and Maid Marian.
My mind palace was replaced with Sherwood
Forest.
'Once More Unto The Breach' circled in my
head like a radio bed;
A million thoughts about those funny, frolicking
fellows layered on top.

Nothing else seemed to matter…

And I used to wonder
The insinuations of a 17-year-old boy
Obsessing over a children's Christmas show…
Daily I worried what that cast of students
must've thought,
Of this scruffy, little weirdo
Who was still singing 'In The Bleak Midwinter'
to himself in May,
And sat in his darkened bedroom drawing them
As drag queens, and playing cards, and last
month's memes…
Daily,
I wondered,
How close they were to filing restraining
orders…

But regardless of whether my social ineptitude
Made me come across as a creepy stalker,
The show really did change my life…
Back to that unnecessary, rhyming exposition:
'I'm not always a happy chappy'.
Frankly, I never was.
Until those magical few hours,
Perched on one of those LPAC, Lego-looking
seats.

I really needed this story.

I needed these characters.
'Marian would be proud of you',
Was exactly the anxiety-shattering mantra I was
missing.
Everyone loved the wandering minstrels for
their eccentricities,
So maybe people can love me despite mine.
When Robin asked Marian for help,
I finally understood that it was okay.
Because if my childhood hero –
And awkward, ongoing crush –
Can admit that he can't face his problems alone,
Then so can I!

Granted,
He's facing the evil Sheriff of Nottingham,
Who would gladly kill him in an instant,
And I'm facing Autism and mental illness
That mostly just makes me twitchy, bad with
loud noises, and cry a lot…
But the point still stands.

I saw myself in Friar Tuck,
The person I wish I was in Will Scarlet,
And what the inside of my head looks like at
3am,
In Eggin, Beggin, Leggin, and Noggin.
I see my struggles now as my own Sheriff,
My friends as my Merry Men.

I'm seeing Hope instead of Chaos,
And I'm seeing Robin Hood…
800 years after he was offed by evil nuns,
In the form of an attractive uni student,
As the man who kicked my ass into gear,
And helped me love life again.

When I'm With You

You know the feeling on a really cold day,
When clouds part for the sun,
And suddenly you're hit by perfect warmth,
That spreads through your whole body?
That's what it's like when you hug me.

You know the smell of petrichor,
After a storm that's so violent,
That you begin to fear the heavens?
That's what it's like when I hold you close,
Breathing the same air,
Surrounded by your sweet scent.

You know when you hear your favourite band,
Or that one special song,
And a little shiver runs down your spine?
That's what it's like when I hear your silky voice.
Even more so when you sing sweet, soothing
melodies...

Your laugh clears clouds,
And paints rainbows across otherwise grey
skies.
I lose myself in your eyes,

As if they were tiny galaxies,
Stretching endlessly into your very soul...
Your soul that is bursting with passion and
kindness,
As your heart beats a rhythm so beautiful,
A rhythm to which the whole world dances,
In perfect, united harmony.

When our lips finally touch,
Perhaps all the romance cliches,
Of sparks flying and stomachs full of butterflies,
Will come true.
As the whole world stops,
And it feels like it's just me and you.

Moments like this I wish would never end.
Like shaking hands clasping pots of ice cream,
As the sun beats down,
And our face paint starts to melt.
Like Skyping til past witching hour,
Until we're so fatigued,
That we just giggle at each other,
Ignoring the rising sun beyond the blinds.

Like strolling around Asylum,
Garbed in goodness knows what,
With smiles plastered on paint laden faces:
Together, Even when not entirely ourselves.

Moments like this I'll never forget...
Because they're ingrained in my brain,
Like files on a hard drive
That can never be wiped.

Cas and Chlöe.
Dean and Krystabelle.
Castiel and Porceline.
Nick and Violet.
Together in this existence and the next,
All because of one tiny spark,
In a conversation online.

The probability of us meeting
Was so infinitesimally small,
Yet we did.
Like fate, or destiny.
No mere coincidence,
As one awkward, strained conversation,
Sparked the flame
That would be kindled into a blazing friendship.
Then a roaring relationship.

People spend their whole lives searching for
perfection,
And I stumbled upon it on Instagram...

We've grown together,
Climbed endless mountains together,

Overcome so many obstacles.
Even if we've had to give each other a leg up,
Or offer a hand along the way.
It's like we've run a marathon,
And when I couldn't quite clear a hurdle on my
own,
You'd come and kick it down for me,
Making sure I make it.
And I hope I've been able to do the same for
you.

Deep conversations from 345 miles apart,
Two twits staring at phone screens,
But hearts and minds never so alive.

Mindless chatter but filled with unrelenting
passion,
As we lose ourselves in the words of the other,
Until we drift off to sleep,
Wherever we happened to be.

Chuckles over FaceTime at 3am,
As we try to keep our voices down,
But just being in the others company
Is enough to cause a grin to spread across our
faces.

Snarky comments about the internet's copiers
and creeps,

Shared in secret
To laugh about as if they were the greatest jokes
ever told.

A relationship unmatched by any other,
Because I fell in love with a very close friend,
And she was in love with me too.

All this sounds like a fan fiction,
Or a shoddy romance novel,
But no.
This is the world through my eyes,
When I'm with you...

I Wish

I wish life was easier.
 I wish I was a stronger person.
I wish my brain functioned properly.
I wish my boobs didn't make me cry.
I wish I could walk where I once did without
being filled with irrational panic.
I wish I was normal.
I wish...

I wish you'd stop joking
About my very real condition,
That can make life a hell on Earth,
Before quickly covering your back with:
'It's just a laugh, it's not about you.'
As if I find remarks about the very way I'm
wired
The peak of comedy.

I wish I was 'typical'.
That's how they describe people who aren't like
me,
And never has normality been so enticing.
I dream of waking up and not losing my breath
When it's too loud, or bright, or crowded.

Of being able to hold a conversation with a
stranger,
Maintain eye contact,
Understand sarcasm,
Understand people,
Understand.

I wish you'd stop saying
That I'm trapped in a girl's body,
When the only thing I'm trapped in,
Is a shitty societal expectation
Of manhood,
And my own, never-quiet, never-calm,
always-whirring, always-hating head.

I wish it were as easily done as said,
To go against the grain,
Against the tide,
Against everything we've ever been told
About who and what we're supposed to be.
But when a guy like me says 'fuck gender roles',
The bigoted majority see the makeup and nail
polish,
And hear 'I'm a lying little girl
Twisting myself for attention.'
So I have no choice but to sit quietly,
And accept toxic masculinity as an involuntary
reality,
And hope to god that society finds the antidote,

Before it's too late for me.

I wish you'd left me be.
Every person who ever caused irreparable damage,
While disguised as someone I blindly trusted,
Someone I loved,
Someone I let into my heart and head,
Who I thought was my world at the time,
And now they're gone,
Whether I wanted them to go or not.

I wish I'd seen the red flags.
If anyone had taken the time to explain them in the first place.
What would life be like if I knew that Dads shouldn't drink that much?
Or that play fighting isn't play fighting if it hurts?
Or that the things he said weren't normal, or okay?
What would life be like if I knew that
A healthy relationship really doesn't involve that much fighting?
Or what gaslighting, guilt tripping, and manipulation looked like?
Or that when they scare you into saying yes it doesn't mean yes,
And that you should get out now...

I wish life was easier,
But god,
Don't we all?
Don't we all...

I wish my different wired brain was better
understood,
Better catered for,
Normalised,
And loved as it is.
I wish gender roles were dead,
And trans wasn't taboo,
And men, women, all those in between or either
side could be themselves no matter what,
So that my boobs could just be 'my boobs',
With no deeper meaning.
Yeah, I wish those people never hurt me,
But more so I wish that talking about abuse was
a normal thing.
That everyone knew the flags, the signs, and
how to get out,
So no one ever has to be hurt like that again.

I wish...
I wish normality was a myth,
And to be unlike any other,
Was the best way to be.
Maybe then,

We'd all see just how strong we really are.

38

Fragmented

We are a white-skinned, blue-haired,
purple-scarred freak.
We are a leading expert in the realm of comic
book heroes,
And the real life loves that have saved so many
more.
We were stripped of childhood,
We are deprived of love,
We are knocked down rather than built up.
We tumbled down staircases and we walked it
off.
We are a genius engineer who can barely pen his
own name,
Or organise his thoughts.

We are 15-years-old, 5 years in a row.
We are a wide-eyed child of the forest,
A portmanteau of fur and flesh: harmonious.
We are a naïve leader of the seasoned
professionals,
Unqualified, unprepared, and unable to back
down from a challenge.
We are an adventurer,
And it's not an adventure if you know where
you're going,

So we are lost,
And we are home.

We are a regret with regrets:
A 'seemed like a good idea at the time',
Whose intentions never produce the right results.
We are Elton John's Saturday night:
'A juvenile product of the working class',
Looking for answers at the bottom of a bottle.
We are broken.
We are riddled with disorder and disease:
Physical, mental, and sexually transmitted.
We are the product of our sins.
We just want to be loved…
But we don't think we deserve it.

We are the last of our kind, but never alone.
We are the guilty party,
Triggering a mass extinction event.
Do we have the right to mourn?
We are a cosmic mystery, an intergalactic oddity,
We are caretaker to the vulnerable…
Enemy to the twisted, and sadistic, and
high-horsed heathens.
We are a true star sailor.
We love you.

We are a juxtaposing jigsaw of abstract parts,
That fit together to fabricate functionality,

And me?
I am but a fraction:
Fragmented yet whole.
I don't know what they are,
But I know their hearts and minds –
Their loves, losses, memories, and mistakes,
For we are one.

Without them,
I am not I.

Rhubarb And Ginger Gin

It was the first time in years,
That the floor was clear enough,
For two to sit comfortably
Side by side.
And so we did.

With near-scentless incense
Filling the air,
Us each nursing a glass of gin,
We rambled:
Endless trivial annoyances,
That meant nothing the next day.
But in that moment,
All was well

The Love Of Nothing

Cups of tea and BBC Ghosts,
Quiet music and naps.
Drag queens watching Twilight,
And cuddles by laptop light.
Double rainbows and one last swan,
Kisses by the pond.
The same lift trip 43 times,
And a dozen 7 minute trains...

I love movies and meals out,
Shopping and cosplay,
But I also love nothing.
The mundane and domestic,
The pasta for lunch.

Not a second with you is wasted.
Every day may not be a grand adventure,
But my heart swells in your presence.
I am calm,
I am happy,
I am the luckiest man alive.

And there is no one in this whole world
That I'd rather do nothing with,
Than you...

Philophobia

Falling…
That's what they call it right?
Falling in love.
As if hurtling towards the earth:
Uncontrolled,
Frantic,
And panicked…
Is somehow romantic?

I don't want to fall in love,
Because I don't want to fall…
I don't want to lose control,
I don't want to hit the ground.
I don't want to shatter…

The heart can only handle so much stress.
You can only bounce back so many times,
Before rubber becomes porcelain,
And the fall leaves you broken…
Rendered unfixable.

No one wants something that's broken.
But that's okay!
That means no one will get close;
No one can make me fall…

It's socially acceptable to be scared of falling.
Less so to be scared of love…
But the heights that make one tremble,
Are equivalent to the friendships forming;
Developing.

The emotions that grow,
Mutate,
Take on a life of their own,
Twist out of control and then?

They wrap around your heart and head.
They squeeze,
They trap,
They suffocate.
They overwhelm and overcome,
Until…
You fall.

And falling isn't like flying.
If not for the lack of control,
Or the permanent destination,
Or the shattering impact…

People run to catch you…
Because hurtling towards the earth
Isn't at all romantic,
But!

The person stood below,
Who opens their arms,
Cushions you,
Takes the force of the fall…
Doesn't want to see you shatter,
Doesn't want you to break,
Puts themself between you and the ground.

Because when we fear falling –
When we fear falling in love –
We fear vulnerability.
We fear opening ourselves to others.
Yet we crave the warmth;
We crave the safety.

And when that person comes,
And catches you when you fall,
It's the greatest feeling in the world.

Legacy

The concept of legacy astounds me.
As a race we are truly obsessed
With creating something confounding to survive
us.
With escaping our outstanding irrelevance.
We clamour for any shred of fame or glory:
Ill-content until secure in the knowledge that in
the far future,
Someone will tell our story.

If legacy really is planting seeds in a garden you
never get to see,
Why do we overlook the blatant truth?
That there is every chance that a round man
With an ugly moustache and no regard for you
effort,
Will ride in on a bulldozer.
Axe down the trees.
Dig up the flowers.
Plant a factory on top.
Drop their legacy and hide you away.
You need only ask Nikola Tesla about his
garden,
Torn up by the man who 'invented' the
lightbulb…

It's a lot of effort to be remembered these days,
For acts of good at least.
Destruction lingers in the mind ,
Far longer than the actions of a modern Messiah.
Devote your life to revolutionising hiccup
treatments,
Or spend one week blowing up monuments.
Roll the dice of remembrance.
Be an attacker or a victim:
All you have to do is kill, or die…

But memories fade…
In centuries to come,
No one will remember the rememberers,
Let alone remember you.
You'll be a life that came and went,
A fraction of a second in relation to all of time
and space.
Because a human being's job,
Is simply to be.
Exist for a while and move on.
Move on to another plane of reality,
Or just cease to exist,
Because it all ends eventually.

It all ends…
Yet each of us seems in love with the idea

Of future generations pasting our faces on
Facebook,
With a set of dates and a paragraph of mourning;
'How they changed the world'.

That's the plan isn't it?
Change the world.
We have romantic fantasies of martyrdom,
But we don't want to die.
Ironic,
Truly ironic…
Legacy lasts not
For those unwilling to make great sacrifice.

When we finally kick the bucket,
Those nearest and dearest will have the clearest
memories…
And when they're gone?
Those who remembered are forgotten,
And the memories continue to fade.
Like ink on the frail pages of an old notebook,
Written by a nameless kid,
With quixotic dreams of his words outliving his
body…

What is legacy…
But an ill-satisfying history lesson,
And a Google doodle ignored by the masses?

Higher Than The Heavens

Once upon a time,
We decided that the universe didn't deserve us.
No gods could judge us,
No systems could restrain us,
No laws could deter us.
Shredding expectations and encouraging
eccentricities,
We decided to live solely for ourselves and each
other.

Chasing our destinies to the ends of the Earth,
We'd kick doubt into the dirt like it was nothing,
Because it is nothing.
We'd tower over it all,
Becoming higher than the heavens,
The second we stopped letting fear control us.
Sliding into the passenger seat,
We gave ambition the wheel,
So we could finally take that back road to
happiness,
In a Reliant Robin fuelled by love.

Ignore the scratches,
And the dents,

And the way the engine rattles,
Because fuck it all!
We're not failing our MOT today,
We've got better things to do.
Better places to see,
Better people to be,
Better lives to live.

A future to rein in,
Because the past doesn't matter.
And in a moment,
Neither will the present.
Failure is fake,
And we are invincible.

The Scene

It's quarter to five on a Tuesday morning.
The drag queen in the DJ box shouts:
Lights!

Despite having watched the sky brighten
From The Terrace,
What felt like only moments ago,
The sudden dispelling of darkness catches me
off guard.
The haze begins to clear,
Drunken dancers dissipate,
Leaving only sticky floors and discarded black
cups behind them.
I turn my attention to the man beside me.
"Everyone's leaving, that's not good."
He confused, and heartbroken,
And absolutely plastered...

He doesn't quite grasp that it's closing,
Instead opting to ask me about 'my plan'.
By that he doesn't mean McDonalds breakfast
and a nap,
He wants to know everything,
And honestly I haven't got a clue.
He accepts my uncertainty;

Nods sagely.
He gets it.

Moments like these are a welcome reprieve
From the absurdity of Grindr natives,
Who've yet to master the art of genuine
conversation.
The lingering crowd is sparser now.
I watch cuffed jeans and high heels shuffle
through the exit,
As a dishevelled bouncer loudly announces that
it's past his bedtime.
Mine too...

My alcohol-infused bench buddy gives me his
blessing.
We met ten minutes ago,
But he's adamant that my future is bright.
He's not the first intoxicated stranger to share
this sentiment,
And as I offer a two-fingered salute -
My wordless farewell -
I hope he won't be the last.

The trek home is 40 minutes uphill,
But after a night of reasonably priced booze and
horrendous dancing
In one of my favourite places,
It's worth it.

And despite the smudged eyeshadow and pit
stains,
This early morning stroll
Is a walk of pride.

Mundane Joy

Find joy in the mundane.
In the way pigeons strut down the centre of the
road,
At 6:23 on a Sunday morning,
No man nor machine to interrupt
Their feathery fashion show.

Giggle to yourself in the middle of
Poundstretcher,
Upon noticing the four pack of apple flavoured,
Shrek branded chapsticks.
It doesn't matter that you're 20 years old.
Buy them for the out dated meme,
Gift them to your friends,
And keep your lips perpetually smoochable.

Dab and floss and whip in 2021.
Drink in the groans of the kids you work with,
Because they think you're 'old' anyway,
So why not crank the dad vibes up to 11?

Race for the back row of seats on the bus,
Because that's where the cool kids sat
On primary school trips.
You weren't cool when you were 7,

You're definitely not cool now,
But it doesn't make it feel any less powerful.

Play bogies in Iceland
When there are absolutely too many people
around for it to be 'appropriate'.
A staple of the British childhood.
Get your mum involved,
And you'll be chuckling next to chicken nuggets
in no time.

Life is too short to limit your own happiness.
Unburden yourself.
Don't let others dull your sparkle,
Because they think childish
Is synonymous with 'bad'.
Find joy in the mundane

The Difference Between Time Lords And Humans

Perhaps the only true difference
Between me in my big, blue box
And you all sat there drinking tea and watching
Corrie,
Is simply that I'm up here,
And you're down there.
Because at the end of the day,
Neither of us really understand how or why
we're here.
And that's ironic,
Or rather appropriate some may argue,
Because monachopsis is a less-than-familiar
sensation:
Alien, even,
But existential crises are inherently human.

Human…
The good old human race!
Spectacularly dull anatomy:
Two eyes,
Two ears,
Two arms,
Two legs,
Two sugars in your coffee –

But only one heart.
If only you could all learn to love as one.
However…

You never cease to amaze an old man:
A really old man…
Because you're so intricately simple –
No,
Your hardware is.
But the software is incredible!
Never in my painfully long life,
Have I met a race that think, and feel, and
imagine
As beautifully as you do.

No other planet has 7099 languages to
communicate between a single species…
7099 ways to describe a rainbow.
7099 ways to word the feeling of warm socks on
a winter's day.
7099 ways to say 'I love you'.

In English alone,
There is a word for the fear that a duck is always
watching you,
And a word for throwing someone out of a
window,
But you're just a simile away from a clinical
addiction to figurative language,

Because you can't concisely capture
How it feels to lock eyes with someone special,
Or the way one sentence can transform an
existence…

You're so charming,
So human.
Sleep is integral to homeostasis,
But it can be inhibited by anticipation alone.
You can forget to shower for upwards of a
month,
But go years without ever forgetting to water
your succulents,
Because 'Laurence Prickard' there on the
windowsill
Is clearly the priority.
You can live on crackers for a week,
Because 'shopping can wait til tomorrow',
But when a hedgehog appears on your lawn
It's a state of national emergency,
Because you've already named him,
And god dammit:
'We need dog food stat! We're not letting John
die!'

You've got monarchies, dictatorships, and
democracy
All trying to pilot this sphere of land,
All at once,

All over the place,
And yet you still can't quite seem to get it right.
Of course,
If you didn't elect infants to govern your
superpowers,
Big, red buttons that make things go 'BOOM'
wouldn't be a concern.
But a salad of ideals
Tossed by kids who think this,
And adults who know that,
Never makes it to the plates of the people.
They never get that satisfaction.

Utilitarianism can only get you so far,
That is if it operates in the first place.
Perhaps that why Utopia
Is such a dystopian concept…
I can only hope you eventually figure it out.

But I digress.
The mighty human race:
You may be stupid,
But you're never boring.
And let me tell you,
Not a single one of you has ever been,
Or will ever be,
Unimportant.

So…

Own your imperfections.
Let go of the past,
Grab hold of the present,
And make your future magnificent.

Shelf Haiku

I was brained by a
Falling shelf which struck my nose!
Decorating hurts...

Recreational Poet

Olivia's got her phone out in class: texting,
Not a care in the world.
I fidget with my phone in my lap,
Laying out the base for a new acrostic under the
table.

Josh is on lookout,
As Bradley slips Beth a fag behind the bike
sheds.
I dodge the gaze of the head,
Before handing out haikus next to the skip.

A hoodie flings his old trainers over the power
line,
Looks around - no one saw;
He hopes to make a pretty penny tonight.
I've left a fountain pen on the fourth lamppost,
I've got odes to spare,
If you've got the cash.

Flashing lights, piercing sirens,
He can run as fast as he can,
But Jordan's busted now,
Caught in the act.
I'm backed into a corner,

They can't take me, not now,
'I promise officer, the sonnets are medicinal!'

I'm part of an underground ring of writers,
Doing unspeakable things with language,
Skulking in the shadows with half rhymes and
metaphors in zip lock bags.
I'm a recreational poet,
And if anyone asks,
I was never here